How They Got Over

African Americans and the Call of the Sea

ELOISE GREENFIELD

How They Got Over

African Americans and the Call of the Sea

ILLUSTRATED BY JAN SPIVEY GILCHRIST

HARPERCOLLINSPUBLISHERS

Amistad

ALSO BY ELOISE GREENFIELD

Africa Dream
Coretta Scott King Author Award

*Childtimes: A Three-Generation Memoir
(coauthor Lessie Jones Little)*
Children's Books (Library of Congress)
Coretta Scott King Author Honor Book
Boston Globe–Horn Book Award Honor Book
Notable Children's Trade Books in Social Studies (NCSS/CBC)
Books for the Teen Age (New York Public Library)
National Council for Social Studies Merit Award Book (NCSS)

For the Love of the Game: Michael Jordan and Me

Honey, I Love

Honey, I Love and Other Love Poems
Notable Children's Books (ALA)
Recognition of Merit Award (George C. Stone Center for Children's Books)
Books for Brotherhood List
A *Reading Rainbow* Selection
Distinguished Books List (Association of Children's Librarians)
Favorite Paperbacks List (IRA/CBC)

I Can Draw a Weeposaur and Other Dinosaurs
Parents' Choice Silver Honor Award

Mary McLeod Bethune
Children's Books (Library of Congress)
Coretta Scott King Author Honor Book
A Classroom Choice (IRA/CBC)

Rosa Parks
Notable Children's Trade Books in Social Studies (NCSS/CBC)
Carter G. Woodson Award (NCSS)

She Come Bringing Me That Little Baby Girl
Notable Children's Books (ALA)
Boston Globe–Horn Book Award Honor Book
Irma Simonton Black Book Award (Bank Street College of Education)
Children's Choices (IRA/CBC)

Sister
1974 Outstanding Children's Books (*New York Times*)

Talk About a Family

Under the Sunday Tree
Notable Children's Books (ALA)
Children's Books (Library of Congress)
Cooperative Children's Book Center Choice Book

William and the Good Old Days
Notable Children's Trade Books in Social Studies (NCSS/CBC)

Library of Congress Cataloging-in-Publication Data
Greenfield, Eloise.
  How they got over : African Americans and the call of the sea / by Eloise Greenfield ; illustrated
by Jan Spivey Gilchrist.
      p.   cm.
  Summary: Profiles African American men and women who have had a strong connection with
the sea, from slaves whose owners sent them to work on ships to today's fishermen, naval
officers, and marine biologists. Includes bibliographical references (p.).
  ISBN 0-06-028991-0 — ISBN 0-06-028992-9 (lib. bdg.)
  1. African Americans—Biography—Juvenile literature.   2. Sailors—United States—
Biography—Juvenile literature.   3. Divers—United States—Biography—Juvenile literature.
4. Explorers—United States—Biography—Juvenile literature.   5. Seafaring life—United States—
Anecdotes—Juvenile literature.   6. United States. Navy—Biography—Juvenile literature.
[1. African Americans.   2. Sailors.   3. Divers.   4. Explorers.   5. Seafaring life—Anecdotes.
6. United States. Navy—Biography.]   I. Gilchrist, Jan Spivey, ill.   II. Title.
E185.96 .G755   2003   920'.009296073—dc21   2002020805

Typography by Matt Adamec
1   2   3   4   5   6   7   8   9   10
❖
First Edition

To those who died during the Middle Passage
and
To those who lived
—E. G.

For Hales Franciscan College Preparatory High School
"In Virium Perfectum"—Unto Perfect Manhood
40 years of taking African American young men "over"
—J. S. G.

Author's Note on Terminology

In reading this book, the reader should keep in mind that, although the word *slave* has been used, no one whose spirit is free can ever truly be a slave.

Also, because the word *Eskimo* is no longer considered by many to be acceptable, the preferred term, *Inuit*, has been used in the chapter on Matthew Henson.

Acknowledgments

For their kindness in granting interviews and providing material, I thank Rear Admiral Evelyn J. Fields, Commander Michelle Janine Howard and Mrs. Shirley Lee.

For his generosity in providing information and material, and for permission to quote the inscription from the *Henrietta Marie* monument, I thank Dr. Albert José Jones.

For sharing their expertise and for steering me to the right sources, I thank Dr. Regina Akers, Acting Assistant Branch Head, Operational Archives Branch, Naval Historical Center, Washington, D.C.; Ms. Janette Graham, Reference Librarian, Black Studies Division, Martin Luther King, Jr., Public Library, Washington, D.C.; Lt. Col. Marilla Cushman and Curator, Dr. Judith Bellafaire, The Women's Memorial, Arlington, Virginia; Ms. Bette Siegel, Documents Librarian, State Library of Massachusetts; and former Seaman Judalon Harris.

For making materials available, I thank the Moorland-Spingarn

Research Center, Howard University; the Schomburg Center for Research in Black Culture, New York Public Library; Lamond-Riggs Branch, Public Library, Washington, D.C.; Greenbelt, Hyattsville, and Oxon Hill Branches, Prince Georges County, Maryland, Public Library; and the U.S. Navy Memorial Foundation.

I am grateful to my son, Steve, my daughter-in-law, Cynthia, and all of my family for their ongoing moral support, and especially to my daughter, Monica, for her valuable assistance during the long months we spent doing research for this book.

Contents

Introduction

How they *got* over, not how they *came* over. Not how African Americans, or their ancestors, came across the water, but, as in the meaning of the gospel song "How I Got Over," how they were able to get on with their lives, in spite of pain, grief and enormous obstacles.

The millions who were kidnapped and taken so far from home that they never saw their families again, the comparatively few who came as settlers, and the descendants of both, got over with courage, ingenuity, spirituality and resilience, the ability to keep coming back and trying again.

For many, many thousands of the descendants of

Africa in America, the getting over has been closely tied to the sea. The lives they chose have placed them where they can see, smell, hear and feel water.

Some were originally sent by their slaveholders to work on ships and remained sailors after they were freed, some were attracted by challenge and adventure, some by the chance to travel or start their own businesses, and some by work that allowed them a little more freedom than the jobs to be found on land.

For others, in modern times especially, it was a career choice that offered, perhaps, advancement and the opportunity to serve. Still others were pushed by their questions and their curiosity to look beneath the sea for answers. But for all of them, there was an attraction to the sea.

The purpose of this book is to show some of the ways in which African Americans over the last two and a half centuries have kept their appointment with the sea. It is hoped that, from these true stories, beginning in 1759 with the birth of Paul Cuffe and ending with the year 2000, a picture will emerge. This picture will show just how broad and deep these experiences have always been in African American life, and their influence on the events of the times.

The sea, with its power and beauty, never begs for attention. It demands it. Humans cannot withhold their fascination with the way it moves and sounds, with its colors, its many moods, its history and the secrets of the earth contained in its molecules.

For this reason, and more, hundreds of thousands of the descendants of Africa have never broken their connection with the sea.

Prologue

More than a hundred African sailors and tradesmen sat in the canoe, the sailors alert and waiting, holding their paddles poised above the water. They watched the approaching wave, waiting for the perfect time to make their move.

The sea held the power, but they knew the sea, knew exactly what they needed to do to keep from being engulfed by the gigantic wave. As soon as they saw the opportunity, they began to paddle furiously, working together in rhythm, pushing past the wave and into the small space of time before the next one arrived.

They, and others like them, lived in the fifteenth century along the African coast, which stretches for hundreds of miles. Good swimmers and boaters, their lives were centered around the sea. Like their ancestors over many centuries, they hollowed canoes out of tree trunks of all sizes to carry fishermen, warriors, and tradesmen and their goods. Some historians believe there is evidence to show that even before the kidnappings began, Africans had traveled to other continents, that they had built boats more elaborate than canoes and used their knowledge of the ocean's currents to take them where they wanted to go.

They spent their days caring for their cattle, taking them to the fields to graze. They farmed, turned the soil and planted, watched their fruits and vegetables grow lush, then traveled by land to trade them.

Living in the interior of Africa, many had never seen the ocean or other large bodies of water until the kidnappings, the long marches in chains to the edge of the continent, and the crossings, the Middle Passage, which seemed to last forever, because the sea was unbearably wide.

They, the kidnapped, from the land and the sea, lay chained together, almost too close to breathe, in the bottoms of ships. Not enough space, not enough air, not enough food, not enough water to drink, they longed for, prayed for, the journey to end and wondered, if they lived, what terrible fate awaited them when they reached the other shore.

How They Got Over

African Americans and the Call of the Sea

PROFILES

Paul Cuffe

1759–1817

The pirates were chasing him, their boat not far behind his, as he sailed out into the ocean. The young man, Paul Cuffe, raced toward Nantucket Island, but the pirates caught up with him and took all his cargo, the items he was hoping to sell in Nantucket at a profit. He returned home to Dartmouth, Massachusetts, to start again. He had to buy all new items to sell on his next attempt.

Almost since his birth, in 1759 on Cuttyhunk Island, just off the coast of Massachusetts, the sea had been a part of Paul Cuffe's life. His father, Kofi, had been a small boy, only ten years old, living in Ghana, Africa, when he was kidnapped, taken to America and sold. He was bought by the Slocum family, of Dartmouth, who belonged to the Society of Friends religion, often called Quakers. Kofi's name was changed to Cuffe Slocum.

Some years later, as Quakers became more and more opposed to slavery, Cuffe Slocum was freed. In 1746, he married Ruth Moses, a Native American of the Wampanoag Nation. The husband and wife earned a living by farming, and over time, they moved to several different places in the area, including Cuttyhunk, finally purchasing a farm of more than a hundred acres in Dartmouth. They had ten children. Paul was the youngest boy and the fourth youngest child.

Cuffe Slocum, the father, taught himself to read and write. He and his wife continued to farm while he built a successful business as a carpenter and builder, hauling items to customers by boat. It was a family business—the children helped, and Paul became very familiar with the workings of boats.

When Paul was about thirteen years old, his father died. The following year, Paul signed on to sail as a crew member of a whaling ship. When that voyage ended, he signed on with cargo ships for other voyages. But the waters were not safe. Americans who had migrated from England no longer wanted to be ruled by British kings, and they had begun their war for independence, the American Revolution, much of it taking place on the sea.

On one of Paul's trips, his ship was captured by the British. He and the other sailors were taken to a British prison. After a few months, they were released because the prison was overcrowded, and were able to return home. At some point during these years, Paul changed his name. Taking his father's first name, Cuffe, as his last, and dropping Slocum, he became Paul Cuffe.

Paul and one of his brothers began building boats and sailing to places that were not more than several hours away, to sell and trade their cargo. Because of the dangers from British ships and pirates, Paul's brother went back to farming, but Paul continued shipping. And that's when he was caught by pirates off Nantucket.

The task was to get from one place to another without

being seen by either British ships or pirates. Sometimes Paul sailed at night. He was robbed more than once by pirates, but he kept trying, and sometimes he was able to make it to Nantucket, where he sold his goods and returned home with a profit.

In Massachusetts at that time, there were serious problems surrounding the rights of African Americans. One of them was the denial of voting rights. In 1780, a small group of African Americans, including Paul, petitioned the state lawmakers for the right to vote. Since they had to pay taxes, they said, they should have the same rights as other citizens.

The petitioners used the same argument that America was using in its war with England: taxation without representation was unfair. Their petition was denied.

America had declared its independence from Great Britain on July 4, 1776, but the war was far from over. It did not end until 1783. That year, Paul Cuffe was twenty-four years old. He had grown up having close contact with African Americans and Quakers, and with members of his mother's Native American family and friends, and the year that the American Revolution ended, he married a Wampanoag woman, Alice Pequit.

Paul Cuffe and his wife lived on their own farm, a very large one, in Westport, Massachusetts. In the years that followed, they had seven sons and daughters. For his children and their many cousins, Cuffe founded a school on his land, and invited other children to attend.

Paul Cuffe's shipping business was a great success. He had built several ships, each one larger than the last. He became known as Captain Cuffe. Eventually, he also began to purchase ships. He added his sister's husband as a business partner and employed his sons, nephews and sons-in-law, as well as other African Americans, as crew members on the ships and to help run the business.

With several ships, Captain Cuffe was able to sail or send his ships to Europe, Canada and Africa, and to many ports in the United States. He and his crews traded goods and caught and sold fish. They also hunted whales, an endeavor that was not frowned upon at that time.

When they traveled to the southern United States, their presence was not welcomed by slaveholders. The slaveholders were afraid that after seeing African Americans who were free, even more of their slaves than before would rebel or run away.

Paul Cuffe had long been aware of the horrors of slavery and of discrimination against free African American people. The first Fugitive Slave Act, passed by Congress in 1793, made life more dangerous for African Americans. Slave catchers were paid well to pursue and capture runaway slaves, not only in the South but also in the North, from where they could be returned South. Often black people who had purchased their freedom, or who had never been slaves, were kidnapped on the pretense that they were runaways and sold to slaveholders in the South.

On his trips to various American cities and to England, and also at home in Massachusetts, Cuffe met abolitionists, people who had formed organizations to push for an end to the practice of slavery. In some of the organizations, all of the members were black. In others most of the members were white. Because he was in full agreement with abolitionists that the system of slavery had to be destroyed, Cuffe was happy to meet with them and discuss ways of accomplishing that goal.

Since his childhood, when Cuffe had attended Quaker meetings with his parents, he had maintained a close association with that religion. He eventually became a member and worked closely with the Quakers on religious matters and on the issue of slavery, although there was a contradiction in the Quaker practices: They worked to end slavery but enforced segregated seating at their meetings.

In looking for solutions to the problems that African Americans faced, Cuffe became convinced that they should return to Africa. He had been to Sierra Leone and felt that it was a good place to establish a new settlement. He would make his ships available to anyone who wanted to go. His plan was to finance an annual trip for those who were willing to migrate, and to continue his shipping business to connect the economies of the two continents.

As he had done throughout most of his adult life, Cuffe wrote letters to people telling them about his ideas. He discussed his plan with other abolitionists. He had become very famous, and much of what he said and did was reported in the newspapers.

The American Colonization Society, an organization that had in its membership many slaveholders, also, for reasons very different from Cuffe's, wanted black people to move to Africa. The slaveholders wanted to force free people out of America to get rid of their influence on slaves.

In December of 1815, thirty-eight free African Americans, some of them parents and children, sailed, without cost, with Captain Cuffe to Sierra Leone to start a new life. On his return, Cuffe continued to encourage others to leave, but there was never another trip.

Until his death, in 1817, Paul Cuffe never stopped working to improve the lives of black people in America, and to connect them with Africa, either as citizens living on that continent or through trade and communication.

He died at his home in Westport, surrounded by his family. He left for posterity many letters that he had written, as well as those he had received. He also left logs, journals he kept during his voyages, that relate daily information about the weather, the direction in which the ship was traveling, illnesses of the crew, and other details.

In 1820, three years after Paul Cuffe's death, eighty-six African Americans sailed to Africa, under the auspices of the American Colonization Society, to start a colony that would eventually become the country of Liberia. Some who went were slaves who were freed only on the condition that they leave America and become a part of this colony.

James Forten

1766–1842

James loved sails. He loved the way they looked when they caught the wind and held it, moving the ships up and down the Delaware River near his home. He lived in Philadelphia, Pennsylvania, where he was born free on September 2, 1766, inheriting his freedom from his parents, Thomas and Sarah Forten.

Thomas Forten's grandfather had been kidnapped in Africa and brought to America on a slave ship. Thomas' father, also held as a slave, had been allowed by the slaveholder to work nights, at the end of each long day of forced labor, and earn money. Most of his earnings had to be turned over to the slaveholder, but a small part of it belonged to Thomas, and he finally saved enough to buy freedom for himself and his wife.

At the time of James' childhood, Philadelphia was a place where there were many free blacks, but also many who were enslaved. The shipping industry was thriving there, and at the docks, James could see black and white workers. He saw black sailors getting on and off the ships, and black stevedores loading and unloading cargo.

When he was seven or eight years old, James began helping out once in a while at the loft where his father worked as a sail maker. Shipowners paid the sail-making company, owned by Robert Bridges, to make new sails and repair torn sails, then bring them to the ships and install them on the tall masts. James waxed the heavy thread that was used by the sailmakers to sew the huge canvas sheets. But James was not allowed to help out often. His family felt that his education was more important.

James attended the free school that had been founded for black children by Anthony Benezet, a member of the Quaker religion. He was James' teacher, and James was a good student. But schooling lasted only a year or two for him. His father fell from a ship, perhaps while climbing a mast to install a sail, and he died, leaving his family sad and without financial support.

At the age of nine, James left school to work and support his mother and sister. He wanted to work at the loft, but he wasn't old enough to be an apprentice, an employee who is paid while learning the skills of a trade. He found a job at a grocery store, delivering groceries and helping to keep the store clean.

Wherever he went in Philadelphia, James could hear talk of the American Revolution, the struggle of the American colonies to be free of British control. The Revolution had recently begun, and when James visited the docks to watch the ships and the beautiful sails, he listened to the talk of sailors who had just returned from battle.

Many of the ships he saw were owned by individuals and previously had been merchant ships, carrying goods to sell. Now they were privateers, ships that had been fitted with guns and other fighting equipment. Whenever they captured an enemy ship, it was sold and the money went to the owners and sailors of the privateer.

On July 4, 1776, when James was not quite ten years old, the Continental Congress issued a document that would become famous. It was the Declaration of Independence, declaring the thirteen colonies free and independent of Great Britain.

But the war was still being waged, on land as well as at sea. The well-armed British army was on the march, getting closer to Philadelphia, and in September 1777, James watched as British soldiers marched into the city and took charge. Many Philadelphians, fearing the takeover, had left before the British arrived, but James' family and other poor people had nowhere to go.

As the years passed, James wanted, more and more, to join the war. He wanted to sail the seas, he wanted to help in the fight for independence, and he wanted to help his family with the money he would earn. But his mother refused to let him go. She worried that he could be killed or, if captured, would be sold into slavery in the West

Indies, as had so often happened to other black sailors, and she would never see him again.

But finally, when James was fourteen, his mother gave in and permitted him to leave. He signed on as a powder boy on a privateer, the *Royal Louis*, and soon he was at war, one of twenty black seamen among a crew of two hundred. At the beginning of every battle, James and other boys would run below decks to bring up bags of gunpowder to be loaded into the huge cannons. The boys had to move quickly, running to get more powder whenever it was needed. In the battles, many seamen, both on the *Royal Louis* and on the enemy ships, were wounded or killed.

One day, not very long after James went to war, his ship was surrounded by three British ships, more than it could possibly fight. The *Royal Louis* surrendered, and all its crew were taken as prisoners.

James, now a prisoner on the *Amphyon*, was sure that he would be sold into slavery. But, as he would tell the story many times throughout his life, his marbles saved him from that fate. He had been the marble champion of his Philadelphia neighborhood and had brought his marbles to sea with him. When Captain Beasly of the *Amphyon* saw his bag of marbles, he told James to play a game with his son, who was unhappy on the ship. As the ship sailed to its destination, the boys played many games and became friends.

Captain Beasly invited James to come to England with him and offered to pay for his education. But James refused, believing it would be an act of treachery to his fellow seamen and to America.

At first, the captain was angry, but then, because James had been a friend to his son, his anger subsided. He decided that, instead of selling James, he would take him where he was taking the white prisoners, to a prison ship, the *Jersey*, which was docked at a New York harbor.

But life on the prison ship, though not as bad as a lifetime of slavery, was torturous. James saw prisoners sick and dying from disease and lack of nourishment. He and the others were imprisoned in the hold, the bottom of the ship, and rarely allowed to come up for light and fresh air. They slept, crowded, on the floor. The food was rotten and covered with mold, and the drinking water was filthy.

After seven months, James was released when some of the prisoners on the *Jersey* were exchanged for some of the British sailors the Americans had captured. When he arrived home, James was so thin that his mother and sister hardly recognized him at first. When they realized it was James, they were overjoyed. They had thought he was dead.

The war was almost over now. America, with the help of France, Spain and the Netherlands, was winning, and in September 1783, the American Revolution ended. America had won its independence. Representatives of Great Britain and America met in Paris, France, to sign a peace treaty.

Several months later, seventeen-year-old James was again on the sea, a seaman on a merchant ship that was sailing for England. The war had not destroyed his desire for travel and adventure.

In England, James worked on the docks, loading and unloading ships. In his free time, he walked around, taking in the sights and meeting people. He heard much talk about slavery and learned that, although it was no longer legal to import kidnapped Africans into England, it was still being done. Africans were being smuggled off the ships at night when no one was there to watch. James was horrified to learn that when he was unloading fruit and other goods from ships, there were probably people in chains imprisoned in the holds.

He heard the talk of abolitionists. Sometimes he went to their meetings and listened to their ideas. He had known about slavery at home, but he was no longer a child. Now he understood more and felt an even stronger loathing for a system that held human beings in bondage.

Later, back in Philadelphia, James Forten became an apprentice at the sail-making loft of his childhood. In a short time, he had completed his apprenticeship and worked his way up to foreman, taking charge of all the other workers.

In 1798, owner Robert Bridges retired, and Forten borrowed money to buy the business from him. Forten was as outstanding a businessman as he was a sailmaker. The high quality of his work attracted many customers. He had invented a sail-handling device that made it easier to lift and move the huge, heavy canvas sails, and as a result, his business prospered. Forten became a very wealthy man.

During these years, Forten had married, but his first wife did not live long. Later, he married Charlotte Vandine, and they had eight children. When their first son was born, he was named James Jr., and Forten became James Forten Sr.

In the meantime, Forten saw every day, all around him, the results of slavery. So many people were not free to live in peace with their families and to be treated as human beings.

James Forten became one of the foremost abolitionists in the United States. His home was a part of the Underground Railroad, a chain of safe houses located in many states, where escaped slaves could hide on their way to the northern United States or to Canada.

He used much of his wealth to purchase freedom for slaves and to finance the trips of escapees. He paid the debts of the *Liberator*, the antislavery newspaper published by white abolitionist William Lloyd Garrison, so that it could continue to operate.

Forten worked long hours in his dedication to the cause of freedom. He wrote pamphlets, made speeches and wrote letters to Congress. He helped to found organizations and met with others, blacks and whites, who were as dedicated as he. Mobs swinging clubs and throwing rocks sometimes attacked them at their meetings.

One of the dedicated people with whom Forten was associated was Paul Cuffe. Forten and Cuffe met periodically to discuss ideas. They wrote long letters to each other and became good friends. Though they remained close friends, Forten disagreed with Cuffe's proposition that African American people should move to Africa.

In 1817, three thousand African American citizens of Philadelphia, including James Forten, held a meeting at

Bethel African Methodist Episcopal Church. They spoke against the American Colonization Society and unanimously passed a resolution stating that free blacks would not desert those who remained enslaved, but would stay in the America their ancestors had helped to build, and continue their struggle.

Forten's children, when they grew up, joined the struggle to end slavery, speaking and writing for this cause. His daughters were active members of the Female Anti-Slavery Society. Some of his children also became well known as poets, teachers and musicians. His granddaughter, named for her grandmother, was the poet Charlotte Forten.

James Forten died in 1842. Between three and four thousand mourners attended his funeral. In a speech made a few weeks later, his son-in-law Robert Purvis, who had worked side by side with Forten as an abolitionist, spoke of his energy, courage and generosity, and called him a good and great man because of his dedication to the cause of freedom for African American people.

Robert Smalls

1839–1915

Robert Smalls, going about his duties on the steamship *Planter*, pretended to take no special notice of the captain and the other white officers as they climbed off the ship to go into the town of Charleston, South Carolina, for dinner and to spend the night, but he was paying close attention. He couldn't afford to make a mistake.

Smalls was twenty-three years old, and he had been considered someone's property, a slave, all of his life. But for the past month, he had been planning his escape, and that of his family and his fellow sailors. Now he had decided that tonight, May 12, 1862, would be the last night that they would be held as slaves. Tonight they would put his plan into operation, and if all went well, tomorrow they and their families would be free.

Smalls had been born into slavery on April 5, 1839, on the McKee plantation in the little town of Beaufort, South Carolina. He had lived with his mother, Lydia, until he was about twelve years old, when McKee sold his plantation and bought a new one near Charleston. Robert's mother was taken to the new place, but Robert was taken to Charleston. He lived in a house with other slaves and worked in various jobs. All of the money he earned belonged to McKee.

In Charleston, a major shipping port on the coast of the Atlantic Ocean, Robert's jobs included many on the waterfront. He worked as a stevedore, loading and unloading the cargo of the ships that docked at the edge of the city. He learned to make sails and to rig them, attaching them to masts and adjusting them. He sometimes traveled on boats as a member of the crews, and when he had the time, he studied maps of the area, learning where the water was shallow and where it was deep, and where there were rocks under the water that could wreck a ship.

In 1856, Robert Smalls married Hannah Jones, who was held in bondage by Samuel Kingman. The couple had a daughter, Elizabeth, in 1858. Smalls wanted to buy the freedom of his wife and daughter so that they could not be sold away from him. When Kingman agreed to sell them for eight hundred dollars, Smalls proposed a new work arrangement to McKee. He said that he would find his own jobs and pay McKee fifteen dollars a month. This arrangement was acceptable to McKee, and though Smalls was sometimes left with only one dollar, eventually he managed to accumulate a small savings.

In 1861, when the Civil War, America's war between its northern and southern states, began, many enslaved men in the South were forced to take part in the fight against the North. Robert Smalls, impressed into naval service, was assigned to work on the *Planter*.

Smalls became the pilot of the *Planter*, but because he was black, he was given the title of wheelman instead.

Nevertheless, he was the one who expertly guided the 150-foot ship through waters he had studied and knew well, transporting guns and other munitions, and soldiers, up to a thousand in number, to wherever they were needed.

In the middle of the night that Smalls decided to carry out his plan, between two and three A.M. on May 13, 1862, he and the other sailors set about the tasks necessary to begin their dangerous journey. They knew that their lives were at stake. If they were caught, they would be killed. But Smalls had not yet saved enough money to buy freedom for his wife and now two daughters. He knew that at any time, at the whim of McKee or Kingman, they could all be separated and never see one another again.

The sailors raised the Confederate flag, the flag of the South, and readied the ship for sailing. Then Smalls put on the captain's hat and stood in the pilothouse, taking the stance of the captain, leaning against the window, arms folded. He had to fool the sentries who stood watch at the several forts they would have to pass, where huge cannons were trained on the water. The forts were some distance away, but still close enough for the sentries to recognize the captain's silhouette.

The ship sailed slowly out of Charleston Harbor. When they reached the Cooper River, they stopped at the boat where their families were hiding and sneaked them aboard the *Planter*. There were now sixteen escapees: eight crewmen, five women and three children.

Smalls was familiar with the signals he had to give in order to get past the forts. He knew the number of times and the manner in which the *Planter*'s whistle would have to be sounded. As they approached each fort, he pulled the cord to blow the whistle, and the sentry gave back the signal that allowed them to continue. Shortly after they had passed the last point, the sentry there realized what had happened and fired, but it was too late. The ship was out of gun range.

Now there was one more danger, this from the Union ships, the ships of the North, that sat blocking the path of any Confederate ship that might try to get through. They, too, had guns trained on the water. The *Planter* quickly lowered its Confederate flag, ran up a white bedsheet as a sign of surrender and steamed full speed ahead toward the Union fleet.

When the crew of the *Onward*, the Union ship that was closest to the *Planter*, saw it approaching, they raised their cannons and prepared to fire. Just in time, they saw the flag of surrender.

Robert Smalls pulled alongside the *Onward* and stopped. He explained to the captain that he had brought a gift for the Union Navy, the *Planter*, a ship equipped with guns and ammunition, worth many thousands of dollars. He had also brought information about the enemy's military plans.

In the North, Robert Smalls was a hero. Newspapers wrote the story of his courage and that of his crew. He and his crew received monetary awards, fifteen hundred dollars for Smalls and a lesser amount for the members of the crew.

In the years that followed, Robert Smalls served as

pilot on several ships and eventually became captain of the *Planter*. After the war ended, he returned to Beaufort, South Carolina, and bought the house that had been owned by the family who enslaved him. The house where he had worked as a slave child now belonged to him.

Captain Smalls became active in politics. In 1868, he was one of many other African Americans who were elected to attend the Constitutional Convention in Charleston to help write the South Carolina constitution. He served in the South Carolina legislature, in both the House of Representatives and the Senate.

In the 1870s and 1880s, Robert Smalls served several terms in the United States House of Representatives. After he left Congress, he remained active in the political life of South Carolina. He died in Beaufort in 1915.

Matthew Henson
1866–1955

There was not one human footprint in the snow. Not one. When the six men stepped onto the northernmost point of the globe, they, and their dogs and sledges, were surrounded by nothing—nothing except snow, and ice, and wind, and bitter, bitter cold.

As far as is known, no human had ever been to the North Pole before April 6, 1909, when Commander Robert Peary, Matthew Henson and four Inuits took the final step of their long, dangerous journey, stood at the very top of the huge roundness called Earth and made history.

The journey had begun by sea, the first leg of it on a ship eighteen years earlier. But in actuality, it had begun

33

long before that, one important part of it with the birth of Matthew Alexander Henson on August 8, 1866.

Henson was born in Charles County, Maryland, forty-four miles from Washington, D.C. He was not born into slavery, not only because his parents were not slaves—they also had been born free—but because the Thirteenth Amendment to the Constitution, abolishing slavery in all of the United States, had been passed the year before Matthew was born.

When he was very young, Matthew moved with his family to Washington, D.C. When he was seven, his mother died, and he went to live with his uncle, who also lived in Washington.

For six years, Matthew attended the N Street School. Then, at about the age of thirteen, he left home and went off on his own, hoping to find work on the sea. He went to Baltimore, Maryland, not very far away, and found a job as a cabin boy, a servant, on a boat bound for China.

After this first voyage, Matthew was promoted from cabin boy to able seaman, a sailor qualified to perform routine duties on the ship. He spent the next four years traveling on the sea, sailing to China, Japan, the Philippines, North Africa, Spain, France and southern Russia.

In the mid 1880s, Henson returned to Washington and found a job as a stock clerk in a clothing store, where, one day, he met Lieutenant Robert Peary, a white civil engineer in the United States Navy. Peary had come into the store to shop. He was preparing to leave on a trip to Nicaragua, in Central America, to supervise other naval engineers in a surveying project. Peary asked Henson to sail with him as his personal servant. Henson agreed, and thus began the long association that would eventually make them famous.

After the trip to Nicaragua, Peary asked Henson to accompany him as his assistant on another trip, Peary's second trip to the far north. Henson accepted the invitation to explore the Arctic region of the world.

In the Arctic, the seasons alternate between several months of daylight with moderately cold temperatures and several months of darkness with extremely cold temperatures. Inuits populated the inhabited areas such as Greenland, but Peary wanted to push farther north, farther than anyone had ever gone.

Henson's first trip north began in June of 1891. The explorers included several men, along with Peary's wife, with Peary as the leader. Food and other supplies were loaded onto the ship that would take them to Greenland, and they left from New York. During the trip, between his duties for Peary, Henson found time to keep a diary, since he was part of the exploring team and not one of the sailors.

The ship sailed as far north as possible, until it reached the place where the sea was no longer water, but ice. There, the explorers were joined by Inuits. Sledges were harnessed to teams of dogs, the supplies were taken from the ship and loaded onto the sledges, and the explorers went to live for several months among the Inuits. The Inuits taught them how to build igloos and hunt for food when their supply ran low. Henson was the only one who became fluent in the Inuit language.

In February 1892, they would begin their trek. Where they were going, they would not be walking on land. They would be walking on the frozen top of the Arctic Ocean.

Their 1891 trip to the far north and the four others that followed were torturous. The explorers walked hundreds of miles, guiding and pushing the heavy sledges, as the dogs pulled. They walked long hours every day in temperatures that were often fifty degrees below zero, sometimes in blizzards where the wind was so violent and the snow so thick they could hardly see. On one trip, Peary broke his leg; on another his feet froze and most of his toes had to be removed.

There were places where the ice they walked on was unexpectedly thin, and they would be surprised by a sudden lead, a break in the ice, leaving water that they could not cross. They would have to wait, sometimes for days, until the water froze again. More than one of the men, Henson and Peary among them, fell into a lead and had to be rescued.

Besides traveling, there was work to be done. At each

stopping point, igloos had to be built before they could sleep. When their food supply ran low, they had to hunt. Broken sledges and harnesses, torn clothes and boots had to be repaired. The dogs, on some trips more than a hundred of them, had to be fed and cared for.

When their 1895 trip was over, Henson promised himself that he would never again leave the warmth and comfort of home. But the next time Peary went, Henson was off again, traveling with him to the Arctic. On each trip, they had reached territory that had never been reached before, a new "farthest north."

In July of 1908, they sailed from New York on the *Roosevelt*, a ship named for President Theodore Roosevelt. Before they left, the President came aboard to wish them well. Months later, they began what would turn out to be their last attempt to find the North Pole. They followed their usual routine of having one group sleep while the other traveled many miles ahead, leaving a trail for the first group to follow, then stopping to build igloos and sleep.

By April 1909, all the Americans, except Peary and Henson, had become ill or exhausted and had been sent by Peary back to the area where they would meet the *Roosevelt.* Accompanied by the Inuits, Ootah, Egingwah, Seegloo and Ooqueah, Peary and Henson continued their journey.

On April 6, 1909, the explorers used a sextant, an instrument that shows latitude and longitude, and determined that they had, indeed, finally reached the North Pole. This story has more than one ending. Some have written that Peary was the first of the six explorers to actually step onto the area called the North Pole. Others have written that Henson and two Inuits, having been sent ahead to make a trail for Peary, who was ill, arrived first by almost an hour.

Most have agreed, however, that Henson was the one on whom Peary relied most to communicate with the Inuits and to gauge the distances they had traveled. Henson's talent for navigation, and the skills he had learned as a sailor, helped him to keep the party moving in the right direction.

When the *Roosevelt* docked in New York, large numbers of reporters and photographers were waiting to interview the explorers. Newspapers had covered the story of their adventures from the beginning, and now that word of their success had spread, people all over the world were waiting to hear more.

The cost of these expeditions, in terms of risk and damage to the bodies of those who participated, was enormous. Many dogs lost their lives, as did at least one man, who, having been sent back to the *Roosevelt*, fell into a lead and drowned.

Whether the goal was worth the risk is a question for each person to answer, but the achievement stands as proof of the endurance and stamina of which the body and mind are capable when it becomes necessary.

After their return, Peary and Henson went their separate ways. Peary returned to his duties in the Navy. He received many awards for his accomplishments. At the time of his retirement from the Navy in 1911, he had been given the rank of rear admiral. He died in 1920.

Henson worked in various small jobs. His autobiography was published in 1912, but very little attention was paid to his achievements, despite the efforts of many who tried to garner for him the honors he deserved. Real recognition was late in coming, some even after his death in New York in 1955.

In 1961, Maryland, the state of his birth, installed in its state house in Annapolis a plaque to honor him as codiscoverer of the North Pole.

In November 2000, Matthew Henson's great-niece, Audrey Mebane, accepted for him the prestigious Hubbard Medal presented by the National Geographic Society.

Shirley Lee
1935–

She skis and bikes and roller-skates, but more than anything, she loves being in the water. As soon as she steps into a pool and begins to swim, her mind goes traveling, and she is often surprised to find that, while she was thinking of other things, she has swum to the other end of the pool. But being under the sea is different. Her mind remains alert, aware of her diving partner and her surroundings, and the rules that have made her an expert scuba diver.

She dives for the fun of it, for adventure, and in that way, she is still very much like the little girl who was born and grew up in Alexandria, Virginia, not far from

Washington, D.C. Born Shirley Marshall on September 26, 1935, the youngest of four children, she liked to be involved in everything. In her neighborhood, she played marbles and jacks and jumped rope. She liked to draw. She could look at an object, sometimes a face, and draw it. At school, she danced in shows, sang in the choir, played baseball and soccer. She was a cheerleader and a drum majorette.

In the summer, Shirley went every day to a nearby playground where, once a week, the children were taken to play in the pool at Fort Belvoir, in Virginia. One day when Shirley was thirteen, they went, for the first time, to the pool at Francis Junior High School, in Washington. She had never had a swimming lesson, but she had been playing and bouncing in water for some time, and she was sure that if she just jumped in, she'd be able to swim.

She was the first one out on deck, and was about to go into the water when another child came out and saw her. He warned her to wait for the lifeguard, but she refused and jumped into what she thought would be not very deep water. But at the Francis pool, the deep water was in the middle and the shallow water at each end, and she was in trouble. Just in time, the lifeguard came out and saw her. He rescued her, and that was the day Shirley decided that she was going to learn to swim.

She became an expert swimmer at Fort Belvoir, Johnson Memorial and other pools in the area. As she grew up, Shirley worked at swimming pools as a lifeguard during the summers. When she was twenty-three, she married Lovell Lee and continued to work as a lifeguard, and then as a manager of swimming pools. After their two sons were born, she would often take them with her to play in the pool when they were on vacation from school.

In 1966, at a pool she managed in Washington, Shirley Lee met the person who would introduce her to a new adventure, one that would become an important part of her life. Dr. Albert José Jones came often to the pool to swim. When Mrs. Lee asked him about the decorative patches he wore on his shirt, he explained that he had earned them as a scuba diver.

Dr. Jones had been a scuba diver for many years. In 1959, he had organized a group of African American men in the Washington area, taught them to dive and founded the Underwater Adventure Seekers. Shirley Lee asked if he would teach her to dive, and he did.

She had to learn to swim thirty-six laps around the pool with a tank of air strapped to her back, and to swim underwater. She wore a face mask that was connected to the tank, a special suit called a wet suit, a weight belt around her waist to keep her from floating to the top, and fins on her feet.

She had to learn to tread water, moving her feet to keep her body upright and her head above water—both with the help of her hands in the water and then with her hands in the air.

When she had learned all that she needed to know to become a diver, Dr. Jones tested her on her skills, and she passed the test. Then she asked to join the Underwater Adventure Seekers. The men voted her in, and she became their first female member.

Her first dive outside of the pool took place with the group in the Chesapeake Bay in Maryland. She had to carry her own equipment, including a tank that was made of heavy steel in those days, instead of aluminum. But she carried it herself and didn't ask for help from the men.

The divers went into the water in pairs. Each one was assigned a buddy to dive with and to stay with, so that they could help each other in case of emergency. Going down, Shirley Lee felt relaxed and free and happy, as she had known she would, because she loved the water so much.

Since that first dive, she has traveled with the Underwater Adventure Seekers to many places in the world while on leave from her computer job in the federal government. Her husband, Lovell Lee, enjoys traveling with her, although he does not dive.

Shirley Lee has executed more than one thousand dives in waters off the coasts of such places as Haiti,

Morocco, Jamaica, Egypt, Mexico, Bermuda and Curaçao. In Belize, Central America, she dove 140 feet to explore a dark blue hole that was approximately the width of two city blocks. She has visited shipwrecks buried in the sea. She has seen all kinds of colorful fish, coral, conch shells, eels and sharks.

On a trip to the Bahamas, she dove in a place where the sharks are kept well fed and pose no threat to divers. When she dove in daylight, she could see that the sharks kept their distance, but during a night dive in the same area, she was afraid. It was too dark to see them, but she knew they were there.

The divers descended eighty feet, using their flashlights to guide them. When they reached bottom, they turned off their flashlights and held hands until their eyes adjusted to the darkness. Their fins shone in the dark, allowing them to swim and not lose one another. Mrs. Lee relaxed and swam, but she didn't totally forget the sharks that were swimming all around them.

There have been a few times when she faced real danger. Once, she was riding in a small motorboat with three other divers when a storm came up. The strong winds blew the waves over the sides of the boat, and it capsized. The divers hung onto the overturned boat as long as they could, hoping that someone would see them and come to their rescue, but no one came. They decided to try to swim for shore.

Mrs. Lee's hands were freezing and her legs got very tired, but she kept swimming, and finally they reached the shore. Later, she discovered that their swim to safety had been two miles long. The stamina she had developed from swimming the required laps around the pool had saved her life.

In all of her dives, Shirley Lee has been grateful to Dr. Jones for all that he taught her—the hand signals to use in communicating with her underwater buddies, how to kick to bring herself up to the surface, to breathe slowly in order to conserve the air in her tank and other skills.

In 1991, Dr. Jones and Miami diver Ric Powell founded the National Association of Black Scuba Divers (NABS), with the Underwater Adventure Seekers as the founding club. Their goal was to organize divers in cities other than Washington to form a network. Since that time, NABS has grown to a membership of more than fifty diving clubs across the United States and in other countries, totaling thousands of divers, men and women.

At their second convention, in Key West, Florida, in November 1992, the members of NABS, in addition to diving, visited the Mel Fisher Maritime Museum. There they saw an exhibit of objects that had been found on the shipwreck of the slave ship *Henrietta Marie*. Shirley Lee remembers seeing the ship's bell, which carried the name of the ship to identify it.

The *Henrietta Marie* wreck lies in the Gulf of Mexico, thirty feet deep, where it had lain for almost three hundred years before it was discovered in the early 1970s by Captain Moe Molinar, a black diver from Panama who makes a living diving on shipwrecks for gold and other treasures. Diving under the auspices of the Mel Fisher Maritime Heritage Society, at the site of what turned out to be the *Henrietta Marie*, Captain Molinar found, instead of treasures, objects that had been used by slave traders.

In 1700, the ship had left London carrying slave traders, who sailed to Africa, captured African men, women and children, took them to Jamaica and sold them into slavery. On the trip back to London, the ship was apparently caught in a storm and wrecked.

Among the most horrifying objects at the exhibit were shackles that had been used to bind the wrists of the Africans. Many of the shackles were tiny, made to fit the wrists of children who had been snatched away from their families and their homeland.

The NABS members felt deeply the pain of their ancestors and wanted to honor them. After the convention, they had a monument made, and in the spring of 1993, a small group of invited members accompanied the heavy, concrete monument down into the water as it was lowered onto the site. On the memorial are words that were composed by member Oswald Sykes:

> HENRIETTA MARIE
> In memory and
> recognition of the courage,
> pain and suffering of
> enslaved African people.
> "Speak her name and gently touch
> the souls of our ancestors."

On May 1, 1999, the Underwater Adventure Seekers, celebrating their fortieth anniversary, presented Shirley Lee with their Lifetime Service Award. Mrs. Lee was proud and happy to receive the award, but it is her love for the sea that keeps her coming back to dive again and again. In order to maintain her stamina and pass the annual recertification test, she visits the pool several times a week and swims one lap after another. In every dive, she must be strong enough to take good care of herself and her underwater buddies.

Whenever and wherever the Underwater Adventure Seekers dive, Shirley Lee will certainly be there.

Evelyn J. Fields
1949–

Every morning on the ship *McArthur*, Evelyn J. Fields arose before daylight. She went to the bridge, the place on one of the upper decks from which the ship was navigated, to find the peace she needed to begin the day. As the ship moved through the waters, she would sit there, looking at the sea, looking out at the stars, undimmed by city lights, and watch the sun rise. She loved the peace of it.

She also enjoyed the fact that she was sitting in the captain's chair. As commanding officer, the person with the highest rank on the ship, Commander Fields was its captain. No one else could sit in that chair.

Evelyn Fields was born in Norfolk, Virginia, on January 29, 1949. When she was a child, living in a low-rent housing project in Norfolk, Evelyn and her sister and three brothers were encouraged by their parents to set high goals. Their parents insisted that they take the toughest subjects and that they do well, and none of the children wanted to be the one who brought home the lowest grades.

Evelyn's parents also wanted their children to be exposed to all kinds of interesting things, such as art and music. Whenever there was a school trip, a choice, for example, between a symphony concert and an amusement park, their mother would make the choice for them. She'd choose the concert, and Evelyn wasn't always happy about that.

In her neighborhood, she played sports and other games with her friends. She learned early how to get along with people, how to work in a group and other skills that she would need later in her life.

Evelyn attended Liberty Park Elementary School and Ruffner Junior High School. It was Ms. Wyatt, a teacher at Liberty Park, who awakened her interest in math and science.

When Evelyn was fifteen, her parents bought a house, and the family moved to a new neighborhood. Evelyn attended Booker T. Washington High School, where her teacher Ms. Brown made math exciting. Evelyn loved the logic of it. It had a beginning and an end, and it made sense.

At Norfolk State College, she continued to study math and science. During her college years, she also enjoyed working at her church, Second Calvary Baptist, with sixth, seventh and eighth graders, as an assistant troop leader with the Girl Scouts.

In her spare time, she went to football games, basketball games and parties. Once or twice, she went to a party instead of studying, but she paid a price for it by not knowing the work, and she didn't do that again.

In 1970, Evelyn Fields was graduated from Norfolk State College with a Bachelor of Science degree in math. Not much later, she joined the National Oceanic and Atmospheric Administration (NOAA) Commissioned Corps. She was commissioned as an ensign, and began a life on the sea that spanned many years. The NOAA Corps, one of the seven uniformed services of the United States, dates its history back to 1807 and is a part of the United States Department of Commerce.

In her first assignment, as a junior officer on the ship *Mt. Mitchell*, Ensign Fields worked as a cartographer. She drew, by hand in those days, charts mostly, but also maps, of the ocean floor. How deep was the water in the areas they surveyed? Were there rocks or other objects that could wreck the ships that traveled there?

The *Mt. Mitchell* was equipped with sounders that sent sound waves down into the water. If the sound returned to the surface quickly, the water was shallow. If it took a long time to return, the water was deep, and a large ship could safely pass. Ensign Fields would record the information on her charts, and the charts were made available to the public so that any ship could use them.

In her next assignment, as operating officer on the ship *Peirce*, Evelyn Fields planned where the ship would go to conduct its surveys, assigned the people and equipment to carry out her plans, then checked to see that everything had been done well.

Her third assignment, as executive officer on the *Rainier*, gave her the responsibility of hiring new crew members, paying the ship's bills and making sure that food and fuel arrived when they were needed.

Her fourth and final sea assignment was as commanding officer on the *McArthur*. Mornings, after she had seen the sun rise and gone to the galley for breakfast, she toured the ship, hoping for a boring day. An exciting day would mean that something had gone wrong, that there was a crisis that had to be taken care of.

She would read the deck log to be sure that everything had gone well during the night while she was asleep. She checked the direction of the ship to be sure that it had not been blown off course by the wind. She read the messages that had come in over the ship's radio, and she read the messages that were ready to be sent out, since nothing could be sent without her approval.

Once a week, there was an elaborate rehearsal for any catastrophe that might occur. Commander Fields often reminded the junior officers to think about the "what ifs." What if this happened? What if that happened? Everybody had to be ready to act.

They rehearsed for fires, putting on masks and fire suits and pulling out the hoses, because, at sea, they couldn't call the fire department. They had to take care of it themselves. Sometimes, at night, they would turn off the lights and pretend that they had lost electricity during a fire. They had to feel their way around the ship, being very careful because the bulkheads, the walls, were made of metal and would get hot if there was a fire.

They rehearsed for the possibility of having to abandon the ship, testing how fast they could put on their life jackets and fasten them, get the life rafts ready, and call the roll to be sure that everyone was there.

The *McArthur* was not a surveying ship. Its mission was science. It traveled to the eastern Pacific Ocean and to Central America, sometimes remaining at sea for as long as thirty days.

On the ship were scientists who tested the sand at the bottom of the ocean for pollution. They studied animal life and fisheries. Commander Fields met with the scientists each day to discuss with them where they wanted to go and what they wanted to accomplish, so that she could give the proper instructions to the helmsman, the steerer of the ship.

One of the scientists' major projects had to do with the protection of dolphins. Whenever the crew of a fishing boat spotted a school of dolphins swimming and leaping in the water, they knew that there were most likely tuna below. The crew would set their nets to catch the tuna, but some of the dolphins were also being trapped. Unable to rise to the surface and breathe, they would suffocate.

When the scientists on the *McArthur* saw a school of dolphins, they would change the course of the ship and follow the dolphins, and by counting the ones they saw, make an estimate of the number in the area. The same scientists returned each year to the same spots to count again, compare the numbers and see whether the dolphin population was increasing or decreasing.

In their travels, there were sometimes severe storms. Commander Fields was fortunate enough not to have been caught in any hurricanes. She and her officers tracked the weather carefully, trying to avoid that danger, but they couldn't avoid storms altogether. The best they could do was to know the ship, know how it rode best, and turn it so that the huge waves hit the bow, the front of the ship, or the stern, the back of the ship, instead of hitting it broadside.

When Commander Fields left the sea, she continued to set goals for herself and move forward in her career at NOAA. There have always been obstacles that she has had to get beyond, some of the same ones, she says, that children often face. Whether it's discrimination against women, or racism, or the jealousy of some people, she continues to hold her ground, work hard and move in the direction she has set for herself.

Now, as Rear Admiral (Upper Half), Evelyn J. Fields holds the highest position in the NOAA Commissioned Corps. Nominated by President Clinton and confirmed, in May of 1999, by the Senate, she is director of both the Corps and the Office of Marine and Aviation Operations.

In her on-land positions, Rear Admiral Fields played an important role in the searches for the plane wreckages of TWA Flight 800 in 1996; John F. Kennedy Jr. and his family in 1999; and EgyptAir Flight 990 in 1999. When the Coast Guard requested the help of NOAA ships, two ships for which Rear Admiral Fields has responsibility, the *Rude* and the *Whiting*, responded and were able to locate the planes. During the search, the admiral kept the news media up to date on NOAA's progress.

Rear Admiral Fields holds many distinctions. She is the first woman and the first African American to reach the position she now occupies. In 1999, she received the Ralph H. Metcalfe Health, Education and Science Award from the Congressional Black Caucus Foundation. In 2000, the United States Department of Commerce presented her with its highest honor, the Gold Medal for Leadership.

As often as she can, Rear Admiral Fields speaks to groups of children and young people, encouraging them to study math and science and advising them to broaden their options beyond the popular choices of professions. "It's a big, big world out there," she says, "and young people should not limit their options."

She still loves the sea. On the walls of her office are paintings of ships and water. "There's a peacefulness at sea," she says, "that you don't get anyplace else."

Michelle Janine Howard
1960–

When Commander Michelle Howard was twelve years old, she watched a documentary about the Air Force and knew immediately what she wanted to be. She wanted to be in charge.

She told her brother that she planned to attend a military service academy, but he said that women were not accepted in those academies. She discussed it with her mother, who said that if things hadn't changed by the time Michelle finished high school, they would sue the government. Her mother explained to her that it was important to fight for what you believed in and that even if changes didn't come in time to benefit you, they would benefit others.

Michelle was born on April 30, 1960, at March Air Force Base, in Riverside, California. Her father was in the Air Force, and the family—Michelle, her mother and three siblings—moved often, following him to the various places where he was stationed. They lived in Guam; California and Colorado, both more than once; Massachusetts; and Alaska.

Alaska was one of Michelle's favorite places. She was in the Girl Scouts there, and enjoyed camping and other scout activities. She went fishing and camping with her family. Her mother took the children to Mount McKinley National Park. Michelle especially enjoyed Sourdough Days, a parade and festival that took place each year in Fairbanks, Alaska.

By the time she was graduated from Gateway High School, in Aurora, Colorado, in 1978, some of the service academies had changed their policies, and Michelle applied for admission to the United States Naval Academy, in Annapolis, Maryland. She passed the difficult interview process and was nominated for the Academy by a congressman. From the thousands of applicants who remained, she was one of those who were selected.

Academy life was strenuous and exhausting, especially the first year, the plebe year. Plebes had to fall into ranks, line up in proper formation, several times a day. Throughout the day, they had classes, followed by sports or marching, then dinner, then study until they heard taps, the bugle call that meant bedtime.

They could watch no television. They couldn't listen to music, or wear civilian clothes. They couldn't ride in cars or taxis or take public transportation. Their only free time was on Saturday nights after dinner. Free time lasted until midnight, and they had to stay within two miles' walking distance of the Academy.

In 1982, Michelle Howard was graduated from the Academy with a Bachelor of Science degree in math. But her education didn't end there. During the years that she has been in the Navy, she has continued to take courses to advance her career.

On the sea, Michelle Howard progressed from being

the officer of the deck, in charge of some of the crew and equipment, to being commander, in charge of everyone and everything, including the mission for which the ship was heading.

While she was executive officer, second in command, on board the USS *Tortuga,* one of her missions was to sail to the Adriatic Sea to support peacekeeping efforts in the former republic of Yugoslavia. She was the first woman in the Navy to be assigned duties as executive officer of a combat ship.

In her last assignment on the sea, Commander Howard was the commanding officer, the captain, of the USS *Rushmore*. The *Rushmore* is a "smart ship." It uses the latest technology and can even be set on autopilot to drive itself. Fewer people are then needed on the bridge, but Commander Howard never allowed the bridge to be left totally unattended, without the watchful eyes of humans.

Along with being a leader come responsibilities. When Michelle Howard accepted the position of commander, in

March of 1999, she also accepted the responsibility that came along with it. It was her duty to take care of the people on her ship. Before taking them into dangerous situations and risking their lives, she had to carefully train them to work as a team. Her failure, or theirs, could mean that some of them would die.

In November 2000, Commander Howard left the sea and went to work at the Pentagon with the Joint Chiefs of Staff.

In her spare time, she likes to read, go trout fishing and collect antique photographs. She and her husband, Wayne Kenneth Cowles, have a dog named Sage.

Commander Howard has received many awards. In May 1987, she received the Secretary of the Navy/Navy League Captain Winifred Collins Award, which is given to one woman officer a year for outstanding leadership. She exults that she has achieved what she set out to do.

She is also very proud of her mother, who, besides working with the organizations her children belonged to as they were growing up, took college courses on and off.

When she was in her late fifties, she received her degree and became a nurse.

Commander Howard remembers the sea with fondness, especially the beauty of moonlight shining on the water. One night, as she was watching the dolphins that were following her ship, bobbing up and down in the water, a sailor standing nearby expressed surprise that, in so many years, she had not become accustomed to the sight. But she never did. No matter how many times she witnessed it, it was always exciting and beautiful.

SNAPSHOTS

Langston Hughes
1902–1967

Many people know that Langston Hughes was a famous writer whose work has inspired children and adults for generations, but not everyone knows that for a time in his young life, he was also a seaman.

Hughes was born in Joplin, Missouri, and grew up in the Midwest. He attended Columbia University, in New York City, for two years, before leaving to spend more time in Harlem, the part of New York City that was heavily populated by black people. He was inspired by the strength of the people, and he wrote about them.

Hughes also spent time on the docks of New York, talking with sailors, and he wanted to live on the sea for a while, travel and see the world, as they had done.

In June of 1923, he took a job as a "mess boy" on the *West Hesseltine* to work in the mess hall, the ship's cafeteria. The ship was bound for Africa, the place Langston Hughes had long wanted to visit. As a mess boy, he served meals and cleaned rooms, but there was plenty of time left for writing, and he wrote about the sea.

Months later, when that trip was over, Hughes sailed twice to Holland, in dangerously stormy seas, doing the same kind of work as before.

In late 1924, he ended his career on the sea. In 1926, he entered Lincoln University, in Pennsylvania, and was graduated in 1929.

Langston Hughes never lost his love for the sea. He traveled the world on ships, first as a sailor, and when he could afford it, as a passenger. When he wrote his first autobiography, the story of his life through his young manhood, he called it *The Big Sea*.

Alex Haley

1921–1992

Unlike Langston Hughes, who began writing years before he became a seaman, Alex Haley became a writer during his life at sea, and at least partly because of it. Haley was born in Ithaca, New York, and spent most of his growing up years in Tennessee. At the age of fifteen, he graduated from high school, attended college for two years, then joined the U.S. Coast Guard.

Aboard ship, he worked as a "mess boy" and a cook. Bored with too much free time, he began to write letters to everyone he knew. Soon he was writing romantic letters for the other crew members to their girlfriends. The letter writing awakened in him an interest in writing stories and articles.

After ten years at sea, Haley was promoted to chief journalist and assigned to an office on land. He retired in 1959 and began to write full-time. His most famous works are *The Autobiography of Malcolm X* and the Pulitzer Prize winner *Roots: The Saga of an American Family*. Among his many honors is the ship the Coast Guard has named for him.

Samuel L. Gravely Jr.
1922–

In September 1976, in ceremonies conducted on board the USS *Reeves*, in Pearl Harbor, Hawaii, Vice Admiral Samuel L. Gravely Jr. took command of the Navy's Third Fleet. In this position, he was, at various times, in charge of 80 to 120 ships.

Samuel Gravely was born in Richmond, Virginia, where he also grew up. After graduation from high school, he attended Virginia Union University, in Richmond, but later left to join the United States Naval Reserve. As a naval reservist, he could live at home and report to the Navy for short periods of time, except when he was needed for active duty.

Sometime after joining the Reserves, Samuel Gravely returned to Virginia Union and graduated. He continued his education while remaining in the Reserves and serving on the sea whenever he received orders to do so. He served in World War II, the Korean War and in other conflicts.

In 1955, he left the Naval Reserve to join the regular Navy. Over the years, he progressed through the ranks. He was the first African American in the Navy to achieve the ranks of rear admiral and vice admiral.

Vice Admiral Gravely retired from the Navy in 1980.

Carl M. Brashear
1931–

Master Diver Carl Brashear, now retired from the Navy, was born in Kentucky and grew up on a farm there. At the age of seventeen, he joined the Navy.

Among the courses Brashear took during his Navy training were deep-sea diving and salvage diving, going under the sea with the purpose of bringing up objects such as the wreckage of ships and downed planes. He became an expert diver.

In 1966, while salvaging a bomb that had sunk off the coast of Spain, Brashear was injured so severely that his left leg had to be amputated. After many months of treatment, he felt he was ready to dive again, but the Navy wanted him to retire. He had to prove to them that he was able to dive.

Carl Brashear became the first amputee diver and the first African American master diver in the Navy. He received many awards and medals, and retired from the Navy in 1979. *Men of Honor*, a movie of his life, was released in the year 2000.

Albert José Jones

(birthdate unavailable)

Athlete, scholar, scientist and educator, Albert José Jones grew up in Washington, D.C. He learned to scuba dive while in the Army. Later, he became the founder of the Underwater Adventure Seekers and cofounder of the National Association of Black Scuba Divers (NABS).

Twice the winner of the Mid-Atlantic Scuba Diving Championship, Dr. Jones has logged more than five thousand dives throughout the world. He is a skier, tumbler and sky diver. He is a sixth-degree black belt in tae kwon do and the former U.S. heavyweight tae kwon do champion.

Dr. Jones holds a Ph.D. in marine biology. He has studied as a National Science Foundation Fellow and as a

Fulbright scholar. Underwater, he researches, photographs and produces videos about the plants and animals that live in the sea.

Along with his work as an official with NABS, Dr. Jones is a professor of marine science and the chairperson of the Environmental Science Department at the University of the District of Columbia, where he also teaches diving.

William Pinkney

1938–

William Pinkney was born and grew up in Chicago. He served in the U.S. Navy and later obtained licenses from the Coast Guard.

While working as an executive in a top cosmetics company, Captain Pinkney bought his first boat. He loved to sail and often participated in boat races.

In 1991, he sailed solo around the world. He kept in touch by satellite with schoolchildren in the United States, explaining his use of navigation, his nautical decisions and the influence of weather on the sea. In 1999, he sailed to Africa and back with groups of teachers, following the route of the Middle Passage, the route that was taken by slave ships.

On July 4, 2000, in a parade of ships sailing down New York Harbor, William Pinkney captained the *Amistad*. This ship, built in Mystic Seaport, in Connecticut, is a replica of the original *Amistad*, which in 1839 was taken over by a group of African captives. In keeping with Captain Pinkney's commitment to education, the new ship will be used as a floating classroom.

Captain Pinkney has received many important honors and is the subject of a video narrated by Bill Cosby. He visits schools across the country and has written a children's book about his trip around the world.

MONIAGE

Civil War Sailors. In a study conducted by Howard University, in conjunction with the U.S. Naval Historical Center and the National Park Service, researchers examined hundreds of thousands of pages of naval documents and found that eighteen thousand African Americans, some of them women, served as sailors in the Civil War. The sailors were remembered in a ceremony on November 17, 2000, at the United States Navy Memorial in Washington, D.C.

The Golden Thirteen. After years of refusal, despite pressure from the NAACP and others, the U.S. Navy commissioned its first African American active-duty officers in 1944. Twelve ensigns and one warrant officer, they became known as the Golden Thirteen.

Inventions. African American inventors were (and are) not uncommon. In addition to James Forten, others have devised inventions for use on the sea. An example is G. Toliver, who obtained a patent in 1891 for a propeller for vessels.

Paintings at Sea. In the early 1940s, while serving at sea in World War II as a member of the United States Coast Guard, renowned African American artist Jacob Lawrence produced a series of paintings depicting life in the Coast Guard.

The Pea Island Station Lifesavers. From 1880 to 1947, on the Outer Banks of North Carolina, the all-black crew of the Pea Island Station of the U.S. Lifesaving Service (later the U.S. Coast Guard) fought stormy seas, often swimming out into the Atlantic Ocean, to save hundreds of lives.

Women Accepted for Voluntary Emergency Service (WAVES). On October 19, 1944, President Franklin Roosevelt approved the Navy Department's plan to accept African American women in the Women's Reserve of the United States Navy. Some of the women would be commissioned as officers. The first two officers were Lieutenant Harriet Ida Pickens and Ensign Frances Wills.

Afterword

A book as brief as this can provide only a sampling of the people, places and occupations that are a part of this enormous story. Perhaps readers will be inspired to travel farther along this road and discover important figures such as Marcus Garvey and Hugh Mulzac; seaports from one end of the United States to the other; and the many men and women who build ships, repair ships, fish for a living, sail for pleasure, operate ships' computers, drive tugboats, treat patients at sea and in myriad other ways answer the call of the sea.

It will be a fascinating journey.

Bibliography

Books

Asante, Molefi, and Mark T. Mattson. *Historical and Cultural Atlas of African Americans*. Paper. New York: Macmillan, 1992.

Bennett Jr., Lerone. *Before the Mayflower: A History of the Negro in America 1619–1964*. Rev. ed. Baltimore: Penguin Books, 1966.

———. *Wade in the Water: Great Moments in Black History*. Chicago: Johnson Publishing, 1979.

Bigelow, Barbara Carlisle, ed. *Contemporary Black Biography*. Vol 5. Detroit: Gale Research, 1994.

Bolster, W. Jeffrey. *Black Jacks: African American Seamen in the Age of Sail*. Cambridge, Mass.: Harvard University Press, 1998.

Brodie, James Michael. *Created Equal: The Lives and Ideas of Black American Innovators*. New York: Quill (William Morrow), 1993.

Cottman, Michael H. *The Wreck of the* Henrietta Marie: *An African-American's Spiritual Journey to Uncover a Sunken Slave Ship's Past*. New York: Harmony Books, 1999.

Counter, S. Allen. *North Pole Legacy: Black, White and Eskimo*. Amherst: University of Massachusetts Press, 1991.

Diamond, Arthur. *Paul Cuffe: Merchant and Abolitionist*. New York: Chelsea House, 1989.

Douty, Esther M. *Forten the Sailmaker: Pioneer Champion of Negro Rights*. Chicago: Rand McNally, 1968.

Farr, James Barker. *Black Odyssey: The Seafaring Traditions of Afro-Americans*. New York: Peter Lang Publishing, 1989.

Gibbs, C. R. *Black Inventors: From Africa to America*. Silver Spring, Md.: Three Dimensional Publishing, 1995.

Harley, Sharon. *The Timetables of African American History*. New York: Simon & Schuster, 1995.

Harrison, Paul Carter, Bill Duke, and Danny Glover. *Black Light: The African American Hero*. New York: Thunder's Mouth Press, 1993.

Haskins, Jim. *Against All Opposition: Black Explorers in America*. New York: Walker, 1992.

———. *Black Stars: African American Military Heroes*. New York: John Wiley & Sons, 1998.

Henson, Matthew A. *A Negro Explorer at the North Pole*. New York: Frederick A. Stokes, 1912.

Bibliography

Hornsby, Alton Jr. *Milestones in 20th-Century African-American History*. Detroit: Visible Ink Press, 1993.

Hughes, Langston. *Famous Negro Heroes of America*. New York: Dodd, Mead, 1958.

———. *The Langston Hughes Reader*. New York: George Braziller, 1958.

Kelly, Mary Pat. *Proudly We Served: The Men of the USS* Mason. Annapolis, Md.: Naval Institute Press, 1995.

McKissack, Patricia C., and Fredrick L. McKissack. *Black Hands, White Sails: The Story of African-American Whalers*. New York: Scholastic Press, 1999.

Meltzer, Milton. *Langston Hughes*. Brookfield, Conn.: Millbrook Press, 1997.

Meriwether, Louise; Lee Jack Morton, ill. *The Freedom Ship of Robert Smalls*. Englewood Cliffs, NJ.: Prentice-Hall, 1971.

Myers, Walter Dean. *Now Is Your Time! The African-American Struggle for Freedom*. New York: HarperCollins, 1991.

Osofsky, Audrey. *Free to Dream, The Making of a Poet: Langston Hughes*. New York: Lothrop, Lee & Shepard, 1996.

Peters, Margaret. *The Ebony Book of Black Achievement, New Revised Edition*. Chicago: Johnson Publishing, 1970, 1974.

Rampersad, Arnold. *The Life of Langston Hughes*. Vol. I, 1902–1941, *I, Too, Sing America*. New York: Oxford University Press, 1986.

Shirley, David. *Alex Haley*. New York: Chelsea House, 1994.

Smith, Jessie Carney, ed. *Notable Black American Men*. Detroit: Gale Research, 1999.

Stillwell, Paul, ed. *The Golden Thirteen: Recollections of the First Black Naval Officers*. New York: Berkley Books, 1993.

Stuckey, Sterling. *Slave Culture: Nationalist Theory & the Foundations of Black America*. New York: Oxford University Press, 1987.

Thomas, Lamont D. *Rise to Be a People: A Biography of Paul Cuffe*. Urbana and Chicago: University of Illinois Press, 1986.

Uya, Okon E. *From Slavery to Public Service: Robert Smalls 1839–1915*. New York: Oxford University Press, 1971.

Van Sertima, Ivan. *They Came Before Columbus*. New York: Random House, 1976.

Weatherford, Carole Boston. *Sink or Swim: African-American Lifesavers of the Outer Banks*. Wilmington, N.C.: Coastal Carolina Press, 1999.

Wiggins, Rosalind Cobb, ed. *Captain Paul Cuffe's Logs and Letters, 1808–1817: A Black Quaker's "Voice from within the Veil."* Washington, D.C.: Howard University Press, 1996.

Other Sources

Alexander, Kitt. "Legacy: The Life and Descendants of Robert Smalls, America's Forgotten Black Hero." Exhibition, February 2000, U.S. Navy Memorial Foundation and the Naval Heritage Center.

Bibliography

Bates, Bryna L. "Making Waves in the New Navy." *Ebony* 54, no. 11 (September 1999): 102–108.

Brashear, Master Diver Carl, USN, Retired. Interview, U.S. Naval Institute, Operational Archives Branch, Naval Historical Center, Washington, D.C., 1998.

"Flashback." *American Legacy* 6, no. 3 (Fall 2000): 92.

Gravely, Vice Admiral Samuel L. Jr., USN, Retired. Biographical sketch, *2002 Naval Leader Monthly Planner*, Officer Biography Collection, Operational Archives Branch, Naval Historical Center, Washington, D.C.

Purvis, Robert. *Remarks on the Life and Character of James Forten.* Delivered at Bethel Church, March 30, 1842. Philadelphia: Merrihew and Thompson, Printers, 1842.

Ringle, Ken. "The Arctic Explorer Rediscovered." *Washington Post.* November 29, 2000: C1–C2.

———. "Sailor on History's Seas." *Washington Post.* March 23, 2000: C1 and C8.

Rosbrow, James M. "The Abduction of the *Planter.*" *The Crisis.* (April 1949): 106–107.

Russell, Madalyn. "Master Diver's Life Inspires Upcoming Movie." *UnderWater Magazine* 2, no. 4 (July/August 2000): 45–50.

Tidwell, Mike. "The Best Democracy I've Known." *American Legacy* 6, no. 2 (Summer 2000): 30–40.

Wheeler, Linda. "A Slave's All-but-Forgotten Run for Freedom." *Washington Post.* February 17, 2000: B1 and B7.

Index

99

Index